*In memory of my father, who taught me
to hear the poetry of nature*

RS

For the sake of wild and watery places

AH

The Lodge That Beaver Built

Randi Sonenshine

illustrated by
Anne Hunter

CANDLEWICK PRESS

This is the crunch in the darkening wood
of teeth against bark where the willow once stood
on the shore near the lodge that Beaver built.

This is the dam blocking the stream

that slid through the woods like a silvery seam,

protecting the lodge that Beaver built.

These are the yearlings that pile up sticks,

then pack them with mud like mortar and bricks,

repairing the lodge that Beaver built.

These are the muskrats, crafty and bold,

that pop in one day

out of the cold,

sharing the lodge that Beaver built.

This is the musk turtle, burrowed down deep
in layers of mud for a long winter's sleep
under the lodge that Beaver built.

This is the curl of wispy white steam that drifts
from the mound while newborn kits dream,
snug in the lodge that Beaver built.

This is Coyote pawing the mound; he scratches

and howls, but the walls remain sound,

so he slinks from the lodge that Beaver built.

This is the mama hauling a limb
with kits close behind her, learning to swim,
circling the lodge that Beaver built.

This is the goose with a silky black crest,
plucking a frond to cushion the nest
that sits on the lodge that Beaver built.

This is the buttonbush, alder, and sedge

hiding new ducklings from Hawk on her ledge

shielding the lodge that Beaver built.

This is the heron, one minute still,

the next with a fish in his scissor-like bill

in the marsh near the lodge that Beaver built.

This is the moose with rippled brown flanks,
munching on waterweed close to the banks,
wading by the lodge that Beaver built.

This is the flood that blasts through the dam,
pounding the pond like a battering ram,
destroying the lodge that Beaver built.

This is the family swimming upstream
in search of a site for their new house of dreams,
leaving the lodge that Beaver built.

This is the crunch in the darkening wood

of teeth against bark where the willow once stood

on the shore near the lodge that Beaver built.

Sink Your Teeth into These Beaver Facts!

Not Your Average Architect

Beavers can actually change the entire landscape and create a whole new eco-system! That's why ecologists call them eco-engineers and consider beavers a keystone species, an animal that others depend on for their survival. When beavers build a dam in running water like a stream, the dam slows the flow of water, creating a pond where they can build an island home safe from predators. This new wetland habitat supports many animals and plants, like those mentioned in the book. Beaver dams also benefit humans by filtering water that runs downstream.

Island Getaway

Beaver lodges are more than just a pile of sticks. They are complex structures with many features that keep the beavers safe and comfortable. Thick layers of mud regulate the temperature in the lodge year-round, and a chimney-like hole in the roof

lets fresh air in and steam out. Several underwater slides allow the beavers to enter and exit the lodge quickly if predators like coyotes or otters get too close. The floor of the main chamber, which is above the water level, is covered with wood shavings. This fluffy carpet not only makes a comfy bed; it also soaks up any water the kits and yearlings might forget to shake off at the door!

Chop, Drag, Stack, Pack, Repeat!

Beavers easily live up to the expression "busy as a beaver." Mostly nocturnal, they spend the nighttime hours from late summer through fall chiseling through trees and branches; digging watery canals to float large, heavy logs and branches to their building sites; and constructing dams and lodges. They also spend a great deal of time munching on twigs, leaves, and watery plants, as well as anchoring lots of leafy branches in the muddy pond bottom to snack on throughout the winter. Then in the spring, they get right to work inspecting and repairing leaks and holes in the dam. There's never a dull moment for these sharp-toothed workaholics!

A Handy-Dandy Tail

A beaver's tail is like a built-in multi-purpose tool! They can use it like a boat rudder to steer them when they swim or like a prop to balance them when they sit. It also stores fat for the winter and makes one whopper of a sound when it's slapped against the water. That comes in handy when they need to warn one another that a predator is near or get the attention of some naughty kits!

Terrific Teeth

What's orange, self-sharpening, and constantly growing? Beaver teeth, of course! The bright orange color comes from the iron-rich enamel, or protective tooth covering. Not only does the iron make beaver teeth stronger, but it also resists acid and prevents tooth decay. Scientists have been so impressed by this adaptation that they are studying beaver teeth in order to find ways to detect and prevent tooth decay in humans.

All in the Family

Beaver pairs have one litter of three or four kits each year, and kits usually stay with their parents for up to two years. Add that up, and you'll discover that there could be as many as twelve family members living together at one time! A large family does have advantages, however; the older yearlings provide a strong workforce, and the younger ones make good babysitters and groomers for the new kits!

A Handy-Dandy Tail

A beaver's tail is like a built-in multi-purpose tool! They can use it like a boat rudder to steer them when they swim or like a prop to balance them when they sit. It also stores fat for the winter and makes one whopper of a sound when it's slapped against the water. That comes in handy when they need to warn one another that a predator is near or get the attention of some naughty kits!

Terrific Teeth

What's orange, self-sharpening, and constantly growing? Beaver teeth, of course! The bright orange color comes from the iron-rich enamel, or protective tooth covering. Not only does the iron make beaver teeth stronger, but it also resists acid and prevents tooth decay. Scientists have been so impressed by this adaptation that they are studying beaver teeth in order to find ways to detect and prevent tooth decay in humans.

All in the Family

Beaver pairs have one litter of three or four kits each year, and kits usually stay with their parents for up to two years. Add that up, and you'll discover that there could be as many as twelve family members living together at one time! A large family does have advantages, however; the older yearlings provide a strong workforce, and the younger ones make good babysitters and groomers for the new kits!

Glossary

battering ram: a large, heavy piece of wood or metal used to break through doors and walls

crest: feathers on top of a bird's head

flank: the fleshy part of an animal's side, between its ribs and hip

frond: a long, feathery leaf

kit: a newborn beaver

lodge: a beaver's dome-shaped house made out of sticks, rocks, moss, and mud

mortar: a paste-like mixture used for holding building materials together and filling gaps

yearling: an older kit that lives with the family and leaves after two years

Want to Learn More about Beavers?

Websites

"Beaver," National Geographic:
www.nationalgeographic.com
/animals/mammals/b/beaver/

The Beaver Institute:
www.beaverinstitute.org

Beavers: Wetlands & Wildlife:
www.beaversww.org

Videos

"Beaver Lodge Construction Squad,"
BBC Earth:
www.youtube.com/watch
?v=yNA62FrKCE

"How Beavers Build Dams," PBS:
www.youtube.com/watch
?v=yJjaQExOPPY